Probing Deep Space

Secrets of the Universe

Giles Sparrow

WORLD ALMANAC® LIBRARY

Please visit our Web site at: www.garethstevens.com
For a free color catalog describing World Almanac® Library's list of high-quality books
and multimedia programs, call 1-800-848-2928 (USA) or 1-800-387-3178 (Canada).
World Almanac® Library's fax: (414) 332-3567.

Library of Congress Cataloging-in-Publication Data

Sparrow, Giles.
      Probing deep space / by Giles Sparrow.
            p. cm. — (Secrets of the universe)
      Includes bibliographical references and index.
      ISBN-10: 0-8368-7279-7 — ISBN-13: 978-0-8368-7279-8 (lib. bdg.)
      ISBN-10: 0-8368-7286-X — ISBN-13: 978-0-8368-7286-6 (softcover)
      1. Cosmology—Juvenile literature.   2. Outer space—Exploration—Juvenile literature.
   I. Title.   II. Series: Sparrow, Giles. Secrets of the universe.   III. Series.
   QB983.S66   2007
   523.1—dc22   2006009960

This North American edition first published in 2007 by
World Almanac® Library
A Member of the WRC Media Family of Companies
330 West Olive Street, Suite 100
Milwaukee, WI 53212 USA

Amber Books project editor: James Bennett
Amber Books design: Richard Mason
Amber Books picture research: Terry Forshaw

World Almanac® Library editor: Carol Ryback
World Almanac® Library designer: Scott M. Krall
World Almanac® Library art direction: Tammy West
World Almanac® Library production: Jessica Morris and Robert Kraus

Picture acknowledgments: All photographs courtesy of NASA except for the following:
CORBIS: 32 (Bettmann); 38 (Roger Ressmeyer). Getty Images: 6 (Time Life Pictures);
29 (Ted Thai); 40 (Hulton Archive); 43 (Ernesto Burciaga). Topfoto: 11.

Printed in the United States of America

1 2 3 4 5 6 7 8 9 10 09 08 07 06

CONTENTS

Cover and title page: Astronomers capture an incredible array of visible light, ultraviolet, and infrared images using the *Hubble Space Telescope*. In this famous photo, stellar explosions provide backlighting for space dust surrounding an actively star-forming region, known as the Pillars of Creation, of the Eagle nebula in M16.

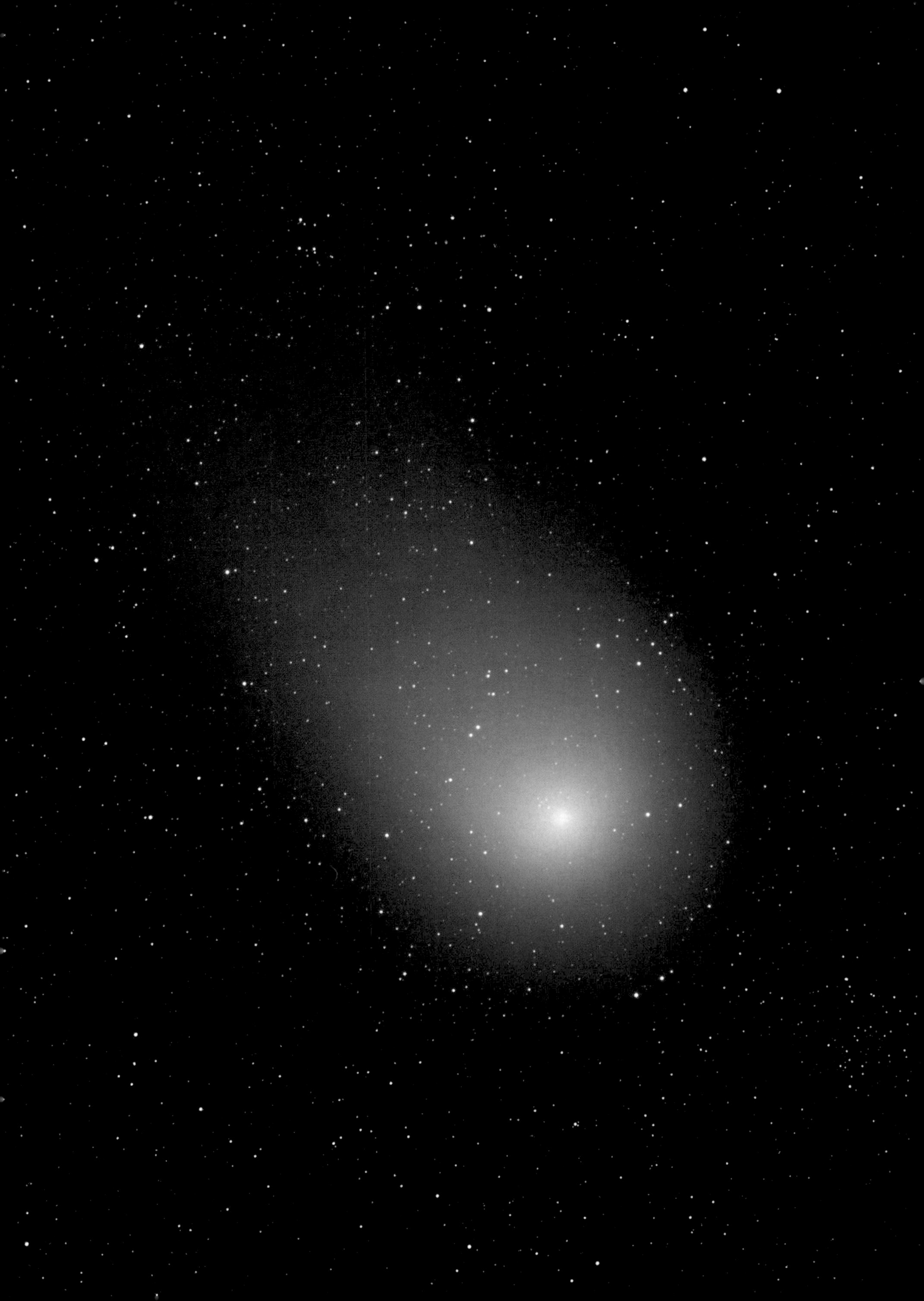

CHAPTER 1

SOLAR SYSTEM MYSTERIES

Although astronomers and physicists would like to believe that they understand how the universe works, much of what they think they know is theoretical. The exciting aspect of dealing with theories is that scientists regularly challenge and test theories as they discover new facts. The new outlook often discredits old theories—which leads to even more theories. Scientists fascinated by the ever-changing mysteries of the universe have the potential to rewrite much of what humans think they know about the cosmos. Yet even in our own solar system—our cosmic doorstep—many unexplained and mysterious phenomena remain.

Fossils from Mars?

Ever since the invention of the telescope, Mars has held a particular fascination for astronomers and the public. In the nineteenth century, some astronomers claimed to see artificial canals on the planet's surface—which turned out to be an optical illusion. In 1938, many Americans panicked when they heard a radio dramatization of H. G. Wells' story of Martian invaders, *The War of the Worlds*, believing that they were listening to a real-life news story.

Today, each new space probe that visits Mars discovers new similarities between the Red Planet and Earth. Most experts now agree that billions of years ago, widespread oceans, rivers, and lakes shaped the martian landscape, and that the planet's atmosphere was thicker and warmer. Much of this water is still there, in a frozen layer of ice just a few feet below the surface, but the surface is now hostile. The big question is whether life ever began on Mars, and whether it might still survive today, despite the tough conditions.

In 1984, the discovery of a meteorite prompted huge excitement. ALH 84001, named after the site of its discovery in

Comet NEAT was discovered in 2004 by astronomers of the Near Earth Asteroid Tracking project, during a search for asteroids that might threaten Earth in the future.

The ALH 84001 meteorite, carrier of the possible martian "microfossils." This lump of rock was easily identified as a meteorite. It could only have reached its resting place among the pristine snows of Antarctica by falling from space.

Antarctica's Allen Hills, is a 4.5-pound (2-kilogram) lump of red rock that was blasted away from the surface of Mars in an asteroid impact. It spun through space for about sixteen million years before crashing to Earth about thirteen thousand years ago. A team of scientists studying the meteorite with an electron microscope discovered that ALH 84001 contained tiny, wormlike structures resembling fossil bacteria similar to those found on Earth. More importantly, their analysis of the rock's chemistry found traces of magnetite, a chemical that, on Earth, is normally manufactured by bacteria.

Although they made headlines at the time, the martian microfossils remain a scientific oddity. So far, there is not enough evidence to prove that they were once living organisms. Critics point out that the "fossils" are far smaller than similar bacterial fossils on Earth and have suggested other ways that the magnetite formed.

THE FACE ON MARS

Mars is a favorite planet for people who believe in astronomical conspiracy theories. In 1976, NASA scientists discovered a hill in the Cydonia region of Mars, photographed by the Viking space probes, that bears a startling resemblance to a human face. Scientists explained the image as an optical illusion created by the Sun's shadows on Mars' topography. Nevertheless, the rumors did not die, and when NASA's *Mars Global Surveyor* went into orbit around Mars in 1997, the agency gave in to the demand for a new photograph of the site. This more detailed image, taken with the Sun at a different angle, clearly shows that the hill is a natural feature. A few skeptics still insist that it was purposely created.

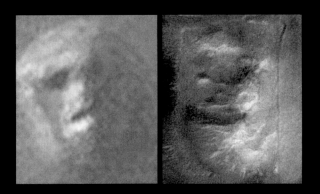

A Viking probe image and one from *Mars Global Surveyor* shows the "face" in detail. They reveal that the distinctive appearance in the earlier image (left) is caused by the angle at which the Sun illuminates this unusual rock outcrop.

Life on Mars, they argue, would be such a monumental discovery that it requires a higher standard of proof than most scientific claims. As a result, this mystery probably won't be solved until astronauts set foot on Mars and start to retrieve and test samples.

Bode's Law and the "missing" planets

In 1766, German astronomer Johann Titius (1729–1796) pointed out what seemed to be a sequence in the spacing of the planets. Another German, Johann Bode (1747–1826), promoted this "law," which became known as Bode's Law or the Titius-Bode Law. The principle became much better known when German-born British astronomer William Herschel (1738–1822) discovered Uranus in 1781, and the new planet turned out to fit perfectly at the end of the sequence. There was, however, just one flaw: There was a "gap" in the sequence between Mars and Jupiter, where another planet should orbit.

In 1799, a group of European amateur astronomers, nicknaming themselves the "Celestial Police," set out to find the missing planet using calculations and observations. They ended up with more than they bargained for— in just eight years, they discovered four small new worlds. These new "planets"—Ceres, Pallas, Juno, and Vesta—turned out to be the largest of a new family of objects that were eventually named asteroids. Most were confined to an asteroid belt in roughly the position of Bode's hypothetical extra planet, known as Phaeton. Many astronomers believed that these objects were what was left of Phaeton after a collision or explosion destroyed it.

Today, we know that the asteroids are not the remains of a lost planet. They are debris from a planet that never had a chance to form. The asteroid belt sits in a region of the solar system where Jupiter's powerful gravity would disrupt any planet in the process of formation. The

Bode's Law used simple math to predict the positions of the planets with surprising accuracy. Titius assigned each planet a number, starting with three for Venus, and doubling it for each planet in turn. (Mercury is assigned zero as a starting point.) Adding four to this number and dividing by ten then gives the distance for each planet from the Sun in astronomical units. (An astronomical unit, or AU, is the distance between Earth and the Sun.) Today, astronomers know that Bode's Law doesn't work for the entire solar system and that it fails to account for the asteroid belt as well as Neptune and Pluto.

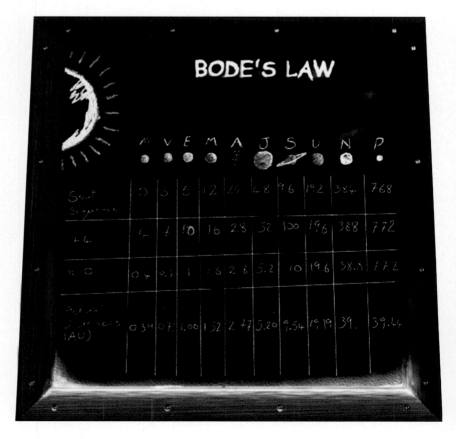

asteroids are, therefore, mostly fragments of planet-forming dust and rock that were prevented from growing above a certain size. There is one interesting exception, called Vesta. Rich in volcanic rocks, Vesta and appears to be part of a broken-up larger world.

Phaeton is not the only "missing" planet of the solar system. French mathematician Urbain LeVerrier (1811–1877), who in 1846 successfully predicted the existence of Neptune from wobbles in the orbit of Uranus, tried the same trick twice more. In 1860, he announced that a small planet or planets even closer to the Sun than Mercury caused wobbles in Mercury's orbit. Several astronomers reported seeing this world, and LeVerrier even named it "Vulcan" (from the Roman volcano god). As time went by, however, Vulcan failed to appear when LeVerrier said it should. Although some astronomers said they saw it, others did not, so many people doubted Vulcan's existence. In 1915, Einstein used his general theory of relativity (*see page 32*) to explain Mercury's orbit without the need for Vulcan, but occasional sightings have continued until recently. Perhaps a small belt of asteroids (nicknamed "Vulcanoids") really does exist inside Mercury's orbit. Despite some investigation, none have been found yet, and searches have ruled out any such asteroids larger than about 40 miles (60 kilometers) in diameter.

Ocean moons?

Another intriguing mystery surrounds the giant Galilean moons of Jupiter, so-called because they were first observed by the Italian astronomer Galileo Galilei (1564–1642). Each is roughly the size of Mercury and has unique features that make it a world in its own right. Io, the nearest moon to Jupiter, is the most volcanically active world in the solar system. Jupiter's gravity squeezes and tugs at the moon's interior just as the Moon's gravity tugs at Earth's oceans. As the rocks are stretched and compressed, they heat Io throughout (an effect called tidal heating). The core remains molten, and sulfurous

volcanoes cover much of Io's surface. The other three moons—Europa, Ganymede, and Callisto—are apparently more placid, but they may all hold an intriguing secret: Perhaps there are oceans of liquid water beneath their surfaces.

The evidence for this is strongest on Europa. Space probe photographs have revealed that it has an extremely smooth, icy surface, crisscrossed with dark lines. There are very few craters,

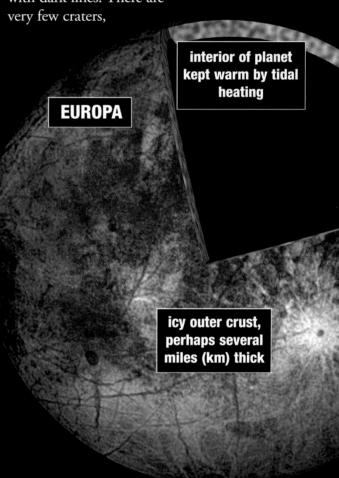

interior of planet kept warm by tidal heating

EUROPA

icy outer crust, perhaps several miles (km) thick

which suggests that the surface is constantly refreshed. The best explanation for these features is that the icy crust is floating on top of a deep ocean of liquid water, kept warm by tidal heating of Europa's interior, similar to the heating that affects Io. Cracks occasionally open up in the crust, and water boils up through them to the surface, where it instantly freezes, healing the gap. Some astronomers believe that Europa's oceans may provide an environment similar to the deep-sea vents in the middle of Earth's oceans, where life exists independently of sunlight. If so, some sort of life may exist on Europa, but we may never know for sure because its crust could be several miles (km) thick.

Ganymede and Callisto are even more mysterious because the evidence for their oceans comes from their magnetic fields, suggesting that these moons have some kind of electrically conducting fluid swirling beneath their surfaces. It couldn't be molten metal because the moons' temperatures are too low, so the most likely conductor would be saltwater. Since these moons are too distant from Jupiter to receive much tidal heating, no one knows why any water there does not freeze.

Mysteries of the outer limits

Urbain LeVerrier's second planetary prediction was of a world beyond Neptune. He believed that Neptune also had unexplained orbital wobbles, and his belief that there was a ninth major planet inspired astronomers for more than a century. Pluto was discovered in 1930 during a deliberate search for the new planet. It is far too small to have any effect on Neptune, so the search for a large tenth planet continued. Recently, new measurements of the masses of Uranus and Neptune have proved there are no unexplained disturbances in their orbits.

Although the existence of another large planet is unlikely, the outer edge of the solar system keeps getting more crowded.

deep global ocean, rich in minerals

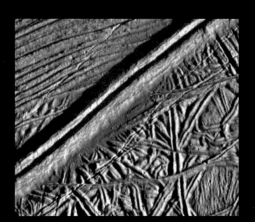

The surface of Europa is covered in dark lines and scars, yet the planet as a whole is extremely smooth. Astronomers believe that the dark lines are created where the surface cracks apart and dirty water wells up to the surface, boiling away into space before the crack freezes over again. A distinct groove is visible in the above image captured by NASA's _Galileo_ space probe. This feature may suggest that Europa's internal structure holds water.

THE SPEED OF LIGHT

All electromagnetic (EM) radiation travels through the vacuum of space at exactly the same speed—186,000 miles (300,000 km) per second. Most often, we call this the speed of light. (What we call "light" is the visible portion of the radiation of different wavelengths that make up the EM spectrum.)

In his 1905 Special Theory of Relativity, Einstein's famous equation mathematically proved that nothing could travel faster than the speed of light. For this reason, we use the speed of light as a "constant"—a unit that never changes. One light-year is the distance light travels in one Earth year, which is roughly 6 trillion miles (10 trillion km). It is a convenient way of measuring the huge distances in space. In other words, a light-year measures distances, not time.

Since the 1990s, astronomers have been discovering new worlds in a doughnut-shaped ring beyond Neptune called the Kuiper Belt. These Kuiper Belt Objects (KBOs) are small balls of rock and ice (called ice dwarfs), similar to Pluto and Neptune's moon Triton. The largest of the new KBOs is actually bigger than Pluto, at about 1,900 miles (3,000 km) in diameter.

The Kuiper Belt seems to tail off beyond the outer edge of Pluto's orbit at about 50 AU (astronomical units). In 2003, astronomers were surprised to find a new world called Sedna. Orbiting well beyond the Kuiper Belt, and as red as Mars, Sedna may be an asteroid, flung out of the inner solar system by a close encounter with Jupiter.

Beyond the Kuiper Belt and Sedna, at the very edge of the solar system, lies the vast Oort Cloud. This is a spherical halo of comets, two light-years across, flung away from the Sun by encounters with the giant planets in the early days of the solar system. The evidence for the Oort Cloud is theoretical, based on the fact that comets with the longest periods (the time it takes for them to reappear to us) often originate in this area. It's unlikely that our Earth-based telescopes will ever be powerful enough to directly detect the Oort cloud.

The Nemesis theory

A few astronomers, however, think that there might be something else lurking out there. During the 1980s, as evidence mounted that the extinction of the dinosaurs was at least partly caused by the impact of a huge asteroid or comet on Earth (*see box, page 11*), some paleontologists (fossil experts) claimed that there was a pattern in these "mass extinctions," with large numbers of species being wiped out roughly every twenty-six million years. Some even claimed that a similar pattern exists in Earth's large impact craters, which suggests that periodic meteor impacts disrupted the environment and wiped out countless species.

THE ELECTROMAGNETIC SPECTRUM

Light that we see is only a small part of the electromagnetic (EM) spectrum—the mostly invisible radiation, or energy, given off by stars. Electromagnetic radiation takes the form of different wavelengths of energy as it travels across the universe. All wavelengths of the EM spectrum move at the same speed: the speed of light—186,000 miles (300,000 km) per second.

The visible part of the EM spectrum, in the middle, ranges from red light (with longer wavelengths) to violet light (with shorter wavelengths). Beyond the visible violet light, the wavelengths become increasingly short, high-energy wavelengths that give off dangerous ionizing, or "hot," radiation such as ultraviolet rays, X-rays, and gamma rays. Likewise, the wavelengths beyond red light become increasingly long, with lower energy levels, such as infrared (heat) waves, microwaves, radar waves, and radio waves.

radio | radar and microwaves | infrared | visible light | ultraviolet | X-rays | gamma rays

If mass extinctions really occur regularly, then what could cause them? The most popular theory is that a very small and dark "brown dwarf" companion star orbits the Sun in a long elliptical (oblong) path. Every twenty-six million years, this companion, nicknamed "Nemesis" for the Greek goddess of divine vengeance, plows through the edge of the Oort Cloud and sends a wave of comets and asteroids toward the inner solar system. If any of these bodies impact Earth, extinctions could possibly occur.

Although the Nemesis theory is fascinating, little evidence supports it. Infrared surveys of the sky's faint, cool objects have failed to turn up the companion star, and many experts doubt that the mass extinctions happen in cycles, or that they are linked to impact craters.

WHAT KILLED THE DINOSAURS?

The extinction of the dinosaurs sixty-five million years ago puzzled paleontologists for centuries. Today, most experts would agree that the impact of a massive comet or asteroid in the Gulf of Mexico was at least partly responsible. The idea was actually suggested by nuclear physicist Luis Walter Alvarez (1911–1988) and his geologist son, Walter (b. 1940). Alvarez's idea was that a big enough impact would have flung huge amounts of dust into the atmosphere, cooling the planet over decades and making it hard for the cold-blooded dinosaurs to survive. This theory only won over the experts when geologists discovered a thin, worldwide layer of the element iridium (rare on Earth but common in asteroids) in Earth's crust. In geologic time, the iridium layer coincides with the age of the latest (the youngest) dinosaur fossils. Paleontologists are still arguing over the importance of such an impact, since the dinosaurs appeared to be in decline at that time anyway.

A landscape of flattened trees surrounds the site where something (probably a comet fragment) struck Earth in Tunguska, Russia, in 1908.

CHAPTER 2

MYSTERIES OF THE STARS

Astronomers today think they have a good grasp on how stars shine and how these objects change size and brightness at different stages of their lives. But there are still many mysterious objects out there, ranging from faint "failed stars" that seem to be common throughout the galaxy, to the super dense and hot remains left behind when the most massive stars die. In recent years, astronomers have also learned to detect planetary systems orbiting stars similar to the Sun, and these discoveries have raised a series of new questions.

Planets of other stars

Astronomers have always wanted to know whether our solar system is unique or whether stars with planets are common in the galaxy and across the universe. We cannot detect planets directly using telescopes, but we can find them by the telltale wobbles they cause in a star's movement (*see box, pages 14–15*). In this way, we have found a huge variety of giant planets the size of Jupiter or larger. This has proved that solar systems themselves are not rare, but systems like ours are rare.

So far, more than one hundred other solar systems have been found. The first to be discovered—a group of three, roughly Earth-sized planets orbiting around the pulsar PSR 1257+12—was probably the strangest of all. They were detected because of their effects on the pulsar's radio signal, which were easier to spot than the orbital wobbles caused by planets circling close to a normal star. Astronomers are still trying to determine how these planets survived the supernova explosion that created the pulsar itself.

Several of the extrasolar planets (planets that orbit stars other than the Sun) have been called "hot Jupiters." They are giant planets orbiting very close to their stars— closer, in fact, than Mercury orbits our own Sun. In the most extreme case, a

Artist's impression of a Neptune-sized world orbiting the red dwarf star Gliese 436. This planet orbits so close to its star that the daytime surface temperature is as hot as the planet Mercury.

FINDING EXTRASOLAR PLANETS

Planets are so small and faint that they are drowned out by the glare of their parent stars in even the most powerful telescopes. Fortunately, astronomers have had a lot of success finding them using an indirect method that measures the gravitational wobbles experienced by orbiting bodies. This relies on the fact that planets don't simply orbit around stars:

A selection of extrasolar planetary systems reveals the wide range of conditions in which planets can survive.

A planet 50 percent larger than Jupiter, with a "year" of 800 days, orbits one of the stars in this binary system. The planet's orbit is apparently stable despite the influence of nearby 16 Cygni A (not pictured).

16 CYGNI B

Three planets orbits a pulsar—the spinning remains of a star that long ago turned supernova. Astronomers discovered the three worlds, each a few times the mass of Earth, by measuring changes in the pulsar's rotational speed. How such planets survived the supernova is a mystery—some astronomers think the planets formed after the supernova.

PSR 1826-11

This sunlike star, 51 Pegasi, is nearing the end of its normal life and will soon swell into a red giant. The planet that orbits it weighs about half as much as Jupiter and orbits in 4.2 days.

51 PEGASI

planet with the same mass as Jupiter orbits the star OGLE-TR-113 in just thirty-four hours. It is impossible for a gas giant to form so close to its star, so astronomers are puzzled about how these scorched planets ended up in such orbits.

Many other extrasolar systems have planets in wild, elliptical orbits. The planets of our solar system also follow elliptical orbits around the Sun, but they are in general much closer to perfect circles. It's a mystery how the extrasolar planets survive in such orbits, where they are much more likely to collide with other planets.

We also used to think that planets would be unable to survive in orbit around the stars of a

Instead, the planet and star orbit around a common "center of mass" called the barycenter. The barycenter is not the same as the center of gravity, but is equivalent to the combined center of mass of all the objects in that solar system. The barycenter is always much closer to a star than to any of its orbiting planets because a star is always much more massive than a planet. In fact, the barycenter is usually inside the star and very close to that star's center of gravity; therefore, the barycenter causes "wobbles" in a planet's orbit around a star. Astronomers measure these wobbles indirectly by analyzing the "blueshifts" and "redshifts" in the light coming from the star. Such shifts in starlight occur as the star moves toward or away from Earth (*see box, page 22*). The sizes of the shifts not only give physicists a rough idea of a star's mass, but also helps them determine the planet's mass and even its distance from the star. Sometimes, the starlight wobbles in several different directions, indicating that multiple planets may orbit that star.

binary (double) or multiple-star system. Because multiple stars are so widespread (more common than lone stars like the Sun), this would have a big effect on the number of planets in the galaxy. It now seems that these ideas were wrong. Several planets have been found orbiting just one of the stars in a widely spaced binary

BROWN DWARFS

The same light-shifting technique used to detect extrasolar planets also revealed an entirely new size class of objects midway between a giant planet and a small star. Called brown dwarfs, these objects are widespread in the universe. A brown dwarf has a mass less than 8 percent that of the Sun. It is made largely of hydrogen and helium, like the gas giant planets and the stars. The smallest brown dwarfs have just 1 percent of the Sun's mass. Brown dwarfs are often found in binary star systems, but are not simply oversized planets—brown dwarfs can even have planetary systems of their own.

Temperatures inside a brown dwarf are not hot enough for the nuclear fusion of ordinary hydrogen nuclei—the process that makes stars shine. Early in their lives, however, they can burn deuterium —a special type of hydrogen that undergoes fusion more easily. Deuterium fusion lasts for just a few million years. Brown dwarfs are generally detected from infrared (heat) radiation generated by the deuterium fusion process.

Gliese 229B (right)— the first brown dwarf to be directly detected, orbits the large, cool red star named Gliese 229A.

system, and there's no reason that planets couldn't form in orbit around both stars of a much closer binary pair (although no examples of this kind of system have been discovered yet).

Cataclysmic variables

Most stars shine with a constant light for thousands if not millions of years, but quite a number are "variables." The light given off by variables changes over much shorter periods. In most cases, the period of time over which the star's light changes allows astronomers to figure out the cause of the star's variation. But some variables are less easy to predict or understand. They often change brightness dramatically and without warning.

Novae (the name is derived from the Latin for "new stars") are the most widespread of this type of star that suddenly increases up to one hundred times or more in brightness for a few days before fading away over the following months. This kind of behavior pattern is called a "cataclysmic variable," and these stellar explosions are actually quite well understood. They happen in a double-star system where one star is a tiny and dense white dwarf (the shrunken core of a star that has stopped shining by nuclear reactions), and the other is a giant

(a dying star that has swollen to enormous size). If conditions are right, the white dwarf pulls hot gas away from the giant's outer layers onto itself, gradually building up into a dense atmosphere. If the atmosphere becomes dense enough, nuclear reactions, similar to those that normally happen in the heart of a star, begin. The atmosphere burns brilliantly until it is exhausted, and the cycle then repeats.

"Flare stars" are another dramatic type of variable. They are smaller, cooler, and dimmer than the Sun, but they can suddenly and dramatically display an unpredictable outburst. These underpowered stars somehow produce solar flares and other activity far more powerful than that seen on the Sun, but no one really knows how.

Other bizarre variable types are the R Coronae Borealis stars. These behave in the opposite way of flare stars and novae. R Coronae Borealis stars shine predictably for years before suddenly losing much of their brightness and taking years to recover. Astronomers think that the drop in brightness occurs when the star flings off a shell of dark and dusty material that slowly expands to hide or dim the light of the star within.

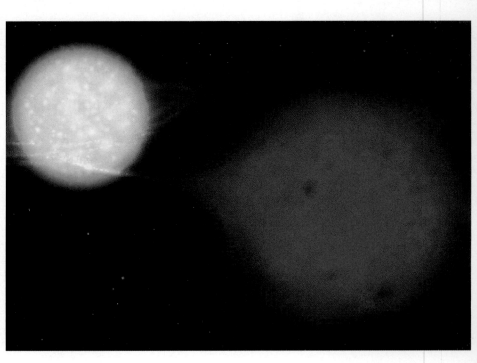

Mass transfer happens when a giant star (right) swells to a point where a smaller companion star with higher gravity can pull away material from its outer layers. The effect is most common with white dwarfs and neutron stars, but can happen with normal stars, as shown here.

TYPE I SUPERNOVAE

Nova systems can sometimes erupt in a spectacular fashion, self-destructing in an explosion known as a Type I supernova. (Type II supernovae are caused by massive stars exploding at the end of their lives.) White dwarfs have an upper mass limit of 1.4 times the mass of the Sun. If the star is any heavier than that, its core will form a super-dense neutron star with a diameter of just a few miles. If the white dwarf in a nova system is close to the upper mass limit, then the extra material it gains can spark a sudden collapse, which causes a brilliant explosion. Because all Type I supernovae always release the same amount of energy and reach the same maximum brightness, they are very useful "cosmic yardsticks" for measuring the distance to far-off galaxies.

As a high-mass white dwarf pulls material away from its companion red giant, hot gas is swept up in the dwarf's magnetic field and funnelled onto its magnetic poles, forming what is known as a "magnetar." If the extra material makes the dwarf's mass greater than 1.4 solar masses, it may suddenly collapse and become a neutron star, triggering a Type I Supernova explosion.

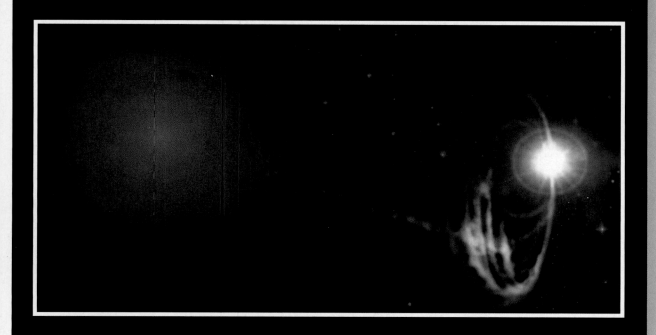

Other strange variables

There are many other types of variable star that still hold mysteries. One of the most bizarre is the star called Epsilon Aurigae. It resembles an eclipsing binary—a pair of stars that cannot be separated with the naked eye. The combined brightness of the two stars drops when one passes in front of the other. Epsilon Aurigae's eclipses happen every twenty-seven years, but instead of lasting for just a few days, they last for two years. This means that the object causing the eclipse must be enormous—equivalent to the diameter of Saturn's orbit around the Sun. But despite its size, the eclipsing object only has a slight effect on the light from the bright star behind it. It is also partly transparent and appears to be doughnut-shaped. The hole in the center allows a certain amount of light through in the middle of the eclipse, allowing Epsilon Aurigae to brighten slightly.

At the moment, the best explanation for Epsilon Aurigae's strange behavior is that the visible star is orbited by a faint companion that is itself surrounded by a huge disk of gas and dust, possibly a solar system in the making. If the companion is also binary, then its two stars might sweep out a clearing in the center of the disk, explaining the brightening in the middle of each eclipse.

SS433 is another strange variable in the constellation of Aquila, the Eagle. It produces radiation of many different types, and Doppler

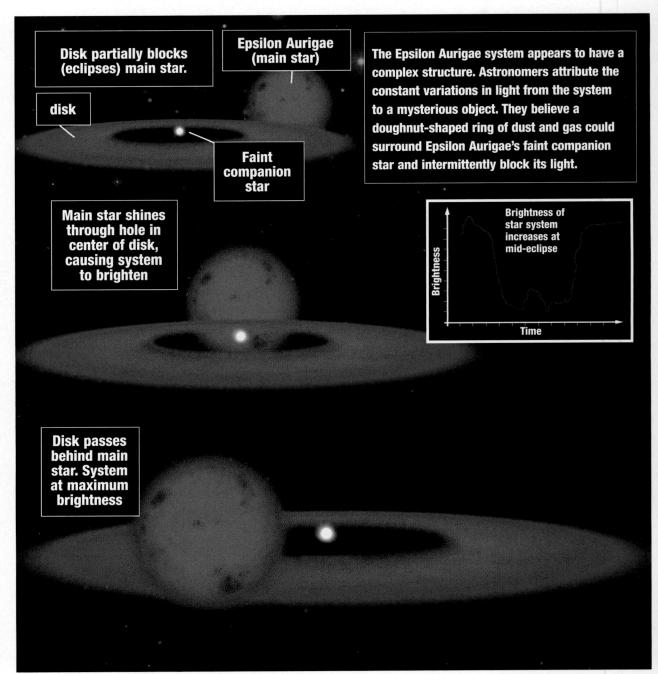

Disk partially blocks (eclipses) main star.

Epsilon Aurigae (main star)

disk

Faint companion star

Main star shines through hole in center of disk, causing system to brighten

Disk passes behind main star. System at maximum brightness

The Epsilon Aurigae system appears to have a complex structure. Astronomers attribute the constant variations in light from the system to a mysterious object. They believe a doughnut-shaped ring of dust and gas could surround Epsilon Aurigae's faint companion star and intermittently block its light.

Brightness of star system increases at mid-eclipse

Brightness

Time

OBSERVING ACROSS THE SPECTRUM

Only a small fraction of electromagnetic (EM) radiation from space reaches the surface of Earth. Although our planet's atmosphere absorbs most of the ultraviolet (UV) and some of the infrared (IR) and radio wavelengths, the visible portion of the EM spectrum makes it to the ground intact. We feel the IR radiation that penetrates the atmosphere as the Sun's heat on our bodies and other objects, while the UV rays that get through often produce skin damage, including tanning or sunburn. Still, the atmosphere also protects us from the more dangerous and damaging EM wavelengths, including X-rays and gamma rays.

We use the different wavelengths of the EM spectrum to explore space. Most ground-based telescopes scan the universe using visible light. For the clearest views, they are often located on mountaintops, where Earth's atmosphere is thinnest. On these mountain peaks, special IR telescopes also detect some of the IR radiation before the denser parts of our atmosphere block it. The best IR observing occurs from space-based telescopes, not only because of the lack of atmospheric blocking, but also because of the lack of ambient heat generated by Earth and by the IR telescope itself—which can distort images. The cold temperatures of space also require less refrigerant for cooling an orbiting IR telescope.

Earth-based radio telescopes, like the famous one in Arecibo, Puerto Rico, consist of huge metal dishes that collect long-wavelength radio waves from space. Smaller versions of radio telescopes, often built in movable groups called arrays, allow astronomers to combine many separate radio images into one larger image. Additionally, space-based radio telescopes collect and beam such data to Earth.

Space-based telescopes capable of studying the universe in different wavelengths became a reality in the decades after the launch of *Sputnik*, the world's first artificial satellite. While the famous *Hubble Space Telescope (HST)* collects images in visible light, it also carries equipment that scans the universe in IR—as does the *Spitzer Space Telescope (Spitzer)*. Space-based UV instruments include the *Hopkins Ultraviolet Telescope*, used by space shuttle astronauts, the *Cosmic Hot Interstellar Plasma Spectrometer (CHIPS)*, and the *Far Ultraviolet Spectroscopic Explorer (FUSE)* Mission. The *Wilkinson Microwave Anisotropy Probe (WMAP)* studies and maps the background microwave radiation of the universe. Space-based X-ray detectors include the *Rossi X-ray Timing Explorer* Mission, and the *XMM-Newton* and *Chandra* X-ray observatories, while the *High Energy Transient Explorer-2 (HETE-2)* Mission and *International Gamma-Ray Astrophysics Laboratory (INTEGRAL)* detect gamma-ray wavelengths. Telescopes dedicated to short-wavelength EM radiation are built to prevent these high-energy rays from simply passing right through them.

shifts in its light (*see box, page 22*) suggest it is moving both toward and away from us at the same time—at high speeds! The only explanation is that most of the star's light actually comes from jets of material escaping from the star in opposite directions. The most likely cause for these jets is a super-dense piece of the remains of a neutron star or a black hole (*see page 32*) orbiting a large old star and pulling material away from it with its powerful gravity. Material spirals in toward the remains of the star, is heated by tidal forces, swept up in the remnant's powerful magnetic field, and then flung away in jets from the magnetic poles.

CHAPTER 3

THE ORIGINS OF THE UNIVERSE

Cosmology is the study of the nature, origin, and structure of the universe—the biggest astronomical mysteries of all time. Modern cosmology holds that the universe began in a "big bang," a huge explosion about 13.7 billion years ago. Evidence for the big bang abounds.

Expanding space

Until the early 1900s, astronomers assumed that the universe was basically unchanging, but that time and space were constant and went on forever. Then, American astronomer Edwin Hubble (1889–1953) discovered that, in general, the further away a galaxy is, the faster it is receding from us (*see box, page 22*).

By this time, astronomers had accepted the fact that neither Earth nor the Sun were the center of the universe. Hubble suggested that the universe is expanding, and the galaxies, including our own, are carried along with the expansion. (Picture the galaxies as raisins in a muffin that rises as it is baked—the expanding dough in between the raisins, or galaxies, causes them to move apart.) If every region of space is expanding at the same rate, then the further apart two objects are to begin with, the faster they will move apart. It's a little like stretching a rubber strip—two points close together move apart less than two points at either end.

The expansion of the universe means that, in the distant past, the galaxies must have been closer together, and the more crowded, earlier universe would also have been hotter. This is the origin of the big bang theory. Belgian physicist Georges Lemaître (1894–1966) first proposed that the universe might have erupted from a compact "primeval atom" in 1933. In the 1950s, Russian-born U.S physicist George Gamov (1904–1968) and others figured out how matter reacted at such high temperatures and pressures and created the modern "hot big bang" theory.

Long-exposure images captured by the *Hubble Space Telescope* allow us to see back billions of years to the period when galaxies first formed.

The big bang

According to the latest data, the big bang happened about 13.7 billion years ago. Time, space, and all matter and energy in the universe were created in that instant. Many philosophers, religious thinkers, and cosmologists have their own ideas about how, why, or what, if anything, triggered the big bang.

The first few minutes of the big bang were packed with activity. In comparison, the remaining history of the universe has unfolded very slowly. Temperatures reached trillions of degrees, and in such conditions, matter and energy switches back and forth.

Albert Einstein was the first person to discover the link between matter and energy. His famous

DISCOVERING THE EXPANSION

Edwin Hubble's groundbreaking discovery came in two parts. When he began his work, there was still debate over whether what he called "spiral nebulae" were small star clusters in orbit around the Milky Way or galaxies in their own right, but at much greater distances. Hubble studied many bright galaxies, looking for Cepheid variable stars—a type of pulsating variable star whose period and true brightness are closely linked. A star's true brightness is the amount of light it emits regardless of its distance from Earth. Knowing the true brightness of the

Cepheids allowed him to determine how far they were from Earth.

Hubble then turned to the spectra of these galaxies (*see below*). The positions of the lines created by individual elements were well known, but in the case of many distant galaxies, they were shifted away from their normal positions. Most astronomers accepted that this redshift was a "Doppler effect" caused by the galaxy moving away from us—a similar effect happens to sound waves; for example, the way the sound from the siren on a emergency vehicle suddenly drops in pitch as it passes. Hubble compared the redshifts with his new galaxy distances, and found that the further away a galaxy, the stronger the redshift effect.

Spectroscopy is the science of studying the different wavelengths of light sources. A prism splits sunlight into a spectrum of colors corresponding to many different wavelengths. Dark lines at certain points in the Sun's spectrum mark gaps where specific wavelengths of sunlight are blocked. The gaps represent "absorption lines" that indicate which element is producing—and therefore absorbing—those wavelengths. The unique set of dark lines on the spectrum of any celestial object acts as a "fingerprint" that identifies which elements an object contains. Astronomers can determine the composition, temperature, and density of an object by analyzing its spectrum.

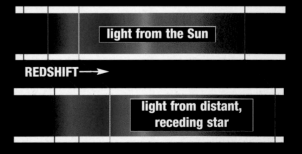

light from the Sun

REDSHIFT ⟶

light from distant, receding star

DATING THE BIG BANG

Although Hubble's Law is universally accepted, astronomers spent decades trying to figure out just how fast the universe is expanding—a figure called the Hubble Constant, or H_0. With an accurate value for H_0, it is easy to trace the universe back to its origins and determine its age.

The difficulty with this calculation arises because, although galaxies across the universe are in general moving away from each other, on local scales (within galaxy clusters and superclusters, tens of millions of light-years across), they tend to be pulled together by their own gravity. With no way of separating the Doppler effects

caused by local gravity from those due to the overall expansion, astronomers found that their estimates of H_0 varied wildly. The only way to determine the constant was to find Cepheid variables and measure the distance of galaxies across a much larger region of the universe than was previously possible. This became the key project for NASA's *Hubble Space Telescope (HST)*, and resulted in our current estimate of the universe's age of 13.7 billion years.

The 7.9-ft (2.4-m) mirror of the *Hubble Space Telescope* is not huge by the standards of modern Earthbound telescopes, but coupled with its viewpoint beyond Earth's atmosphere, it gives the *HST* the sharpest view of the distant cosmos, enabling it to pick out individual Cepheid variables across tens of millions of light-years.

equation, $E=mc^2$ (energy equals mass multiplied by the speed of light squared), means that energy can be converted directly into matter, and matter can be converted into energy. In general, matter particles are unstable and will tend to "decay," breaking apart into smaller particles or switching back into energy. Only a few types of particles—such as the protons, neutrons, and electrons that make up everyday matter—can remain stable in today's relatively cool universe.

Scientists use huge machines called particle accelerators to smash together tiny subatomic particles at speeds close to the speed of light in hopes of recreating the much hotter and higher-energy environment of the early universe. The

energy released in the process briefly forms new and exotic particles. Particle accelerators are the closest we can get to studying the big bang itself. These studies reveal that particles in the universe fall into two basic groups: heavy particles, with masses comparable to those of today's protons and neutrons, and lightweight particles, with masses as light—or even lighter than—electrons.

Most of the heavy particles formed in the big bang were members of a family of particles called quarks. There are six different types of quark in all—called "up," "down," "strange," "charm," "top," and "bottom." Each of these particles is considered fundamental, which means that it cannot be split into smaller particles. The four

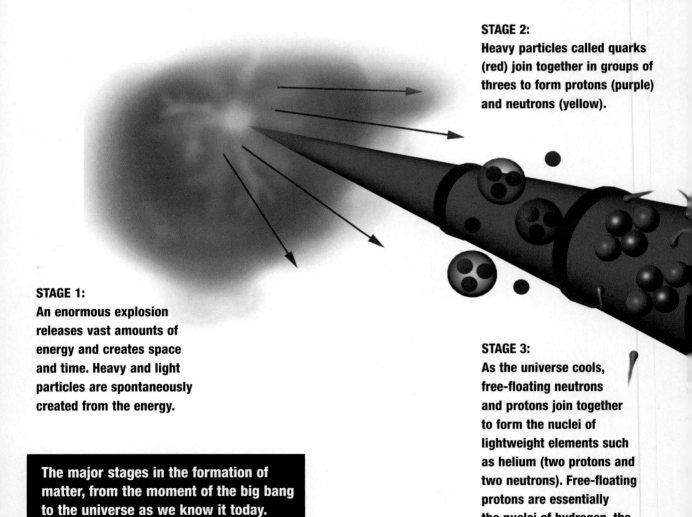

STAGE 2:
Heavy particles called quarks (red) join together in groups of threes to form protons (purple) and neutrons (yellow).

STAGE 1:
An enormous explosion releases vast amounts of energy and creates space and time. Heavy and light particles are spontaneously created from the energy.

The major stages in the formation of matter, from the moment of the big bang to the universe as we know it today.

STAGE 3:
As the universe cools, free-floating neutrons and protons join together to form the nuclei of lightweight elements such as helium (two protons and two neutrons). Free-floating protons are essentially the nuclei of hydrogen, the simplest and most common element in the universe.

heavier quarks—strange, charm, top, and bottom—are unstable in today's universe. Only the up and down quarks are common. As temperatures in the universe fell after the big bang, the up and down quarks joined together in groups of three to create protons and neutrons.

The period of formation for quarks and other heavy, unstable particles lasted for just one-billionth of a second. Still, enough energy remained for a fraction of a second longer to create lighter particles, collectively called leptons. Leptons are similar to quarks in that there are six types—the electron, muon, and tauon, and the electron, mu, and tau neutrinos. These six leptons are also considered fundamental. Only

two are stable at low temperatures: the electron and the nearly massless electron neutrino. By the time one second had passed, temperatures had dropped too low for energy to spontaneously create what we know as matter. The universe was a seething mass of loose energy, with quarks, electrons, neutrinos, and photons of radiation bouncing back and forth between one another.

Even before matter had stopped forming, it began to cluster together. At first, high temperatures prevented any particles from bonding, but at about one microsecond (one thousandth of a second), the surviving quarks were able to bond with each other, creating protons and neutrons in a ratio of roughly seven

STAGE 4:
As the temperature drops further, free-floating electrons (blue) orbit around the nuclei, forming the first true atoms. At this stage (about 300,000 years after the big bang), the universe becomes transparent.

STAGE 5:
Enormous clouds of gas and dust collapse to form the first stars and galaxies, roughly one million years after the big bang.

STAGE 6:
Today, the universe is full of stars and galaxies. Much of its material has been recycled several times by successive generations of stars, enriching the universe with heavier and more complex elements.

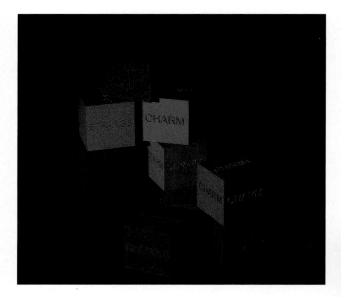

All of the matter in today's universe is made up of fundamental particles, somewhat like building blocks. Only two quarks, the "up" and "down," can exist in everyday matter. The other quarks—"charm," "strange," "top," and "bottom"—may "wink" into existence inside particle accelerators.

At age thirty-two, physicist Alan Guth suggested the inflation theory to explain how the big bang resulted in clumps of matter that formed today's galaxies and galaxy clusters.

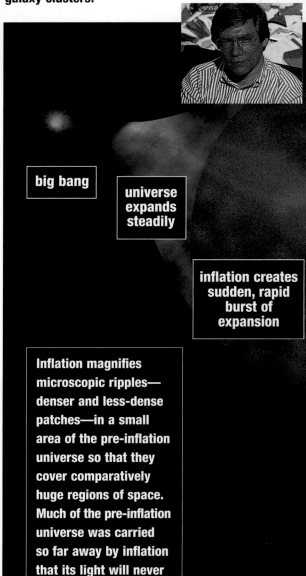

to one. By one hundred seconds, the protons and neutrons were also able to join together, creating the atomic nuclei of simple elements. Most of the protons could not pair up, however, and so remained alone as nuclei of the simplest and most plentiful element—hydrogen.

After about 300,000 years, electrons combined with these nuclei to form the first proper atoms, but not until temperatures dropped below 4,900 ºFahrenheit (2,700 ºCelsius). Up to this point, the universe was so crowded with particles that it was "foggy"—photons of light radition could not travel far without hitting other particles. As the nuclei and electrons finally paired up, the universe suddenly became transparent, and light could travel for long distances for the first time.

Problems and patches

The big bang theory was successful because its predictions could be tested. It accounted for the proportions of hydrogen and other "light" elements (not to be confused with photons of light) formed in the explosion, explained the expansion of the universe, and, most importantly, predicted that the universe should still be faintly "glowing" with radiation left over from the moment it became transparent. This radiation, known as Cosmic Microwave Background (CMB) radiation, was discovered in 1964.

big bang

universe expands steadily

inflation creates sudden, rapid burst of expansion

Inflation magnifies microscopic ripples—denser and less-dense patches—in a small area of the pre-inflation universe so that they cover comparatively huge regions of space. Much of the pre-inflation universe was carried so far away by inflation that its light will never reach Earth.

But there are problems with the big bang theory, and it has been "patched up" several times. The most important of these patches is inflation, suggested in 1981 by U.S. physicist Alan Guth (b. 1947). At the time, cosmologists faced a major problem. On its own, the big bang predicts a universe where we shouldn't exist. All the while the universe was foggy, pressure from the photons bouncing around should have prevented matter from clumping together. When the fog lifted, matter should have already been evenly spread out, which does not explain the strings and sheets of galaxy clusters and apparent voids that appear on our large-scale maps of the universe.

Guth's solution, called "inflation," was ingenious—he suggested that within the first fraction of a second of the big bang, a second enormous release of energy caused a small region of the universe to balloon outward to form the entire universe as we understand it today. Tiny ripples that started to build up in

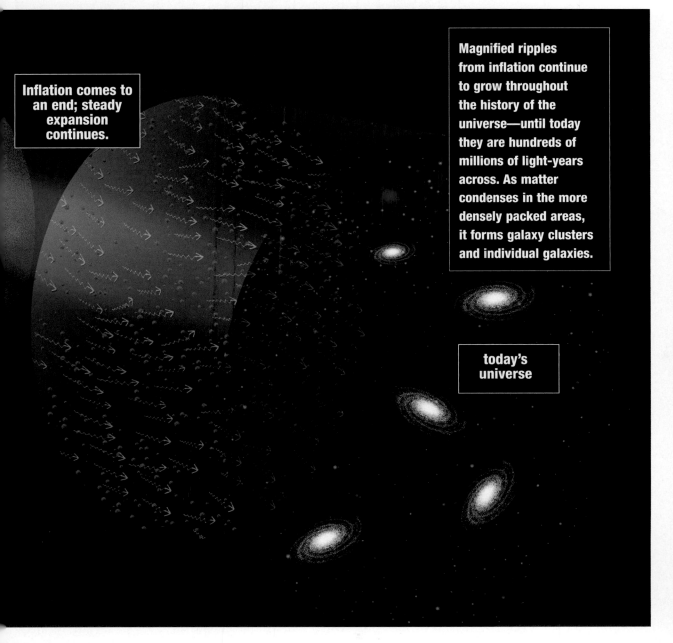

Inflation comes to an end; steady expansion continues.

Magnified ripples from inflation continue to grow throughout the history of the universe—until today they are hundreds of millions of light-years across. As matter condenses in the more densely packed areas, it forms galaxy clusters and individual galaxies.

today's universe

this region of the early universe were magnified enormously, which explains why matter in the universe is not evenly distributed. Guth even suggested that the energy to power inflation could have originated from the fragmentation of a short-lived "superforce" that created the four forces that govern today's universe (electromagnetism, gravity, and the weak and strong nuclear forces).

Although inflation is a complex addition to the big bang theory, it is needed to help explain how the big bang could produce a universe like ours. Inflation received a major boost in 1992 when the *COBE (Cosmic Background Explorer)* satellite successfully detected tiny temperature and density differences in the CMB—the apparent missing link between the quantum ripples of inflation and the structure of the universe today.

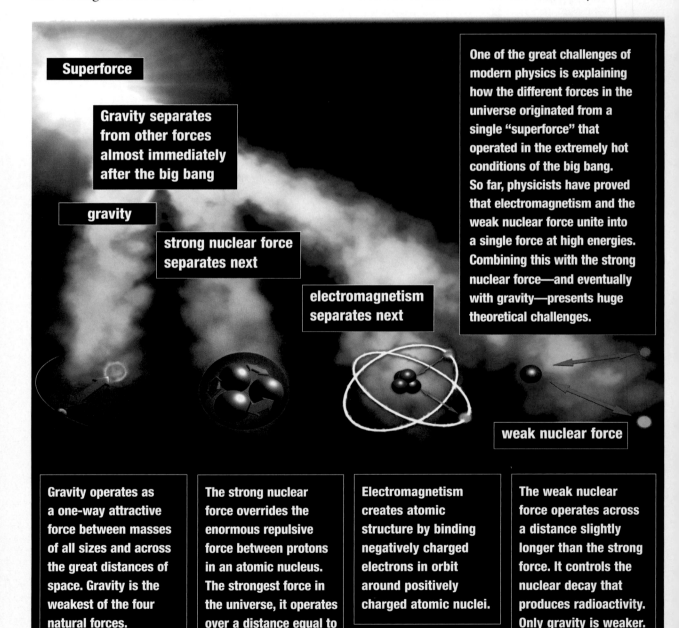

Superforce

Gravity separates from other forces almost immediately after the big bang

gravity

strong nuclear force separates next

electromagnetism separates next

weak nuclear force

One of the great challenges of modern physics is explaining how the different forces in the universe originated from a single "superforce" that operated in the extremely hot conditions of the big bang. So far, physicists have proved that electromagnetism and the weak nuclear force unite into a single force at high energies. Combining this with the strong nuclear force—and eventually with gravity—presents huge theoretical challenges.

Gravity operates as a one-way attractive force between masses of all sizes and across the great distances of space. Gravity is the weakest of the four natural forces.

The strong nuclear force overrides the enormous repulsive force between protons in an atomic nucleus. The strongest force in the universe, it operates over a distance equal to the width of a proton.

Electromagnetism creates atomic structure by binding negatively charged electrons in orbit around positively charged atomic nuclei.

The weak nuclear force operates across a distance slightly longer than the strong force. It controls the nuclear decay that produces radioactivity. Only gravity is weaker.

THE SHAPE OF THE UNIVERSE

How can the universe have a shape? Can something that extends forever in all directions have a shape? And if the big bang 13.7 billion years ago created space-time, what was there before? In other words, what is the universe in, and does it have a shape?

The obvious answer is that the universe is an expanding sphere. In that case, where is the center of the sphere? From our viewpoint on Earth, we seem to be the center. When we measure the speed of distant galaxies, they all seem to be moving away from us. The deeper into space we look, the farther back in time we can see, until thirteen billion light-years away—at the limit of our "observable" universe—we should see all the way back to the beginning of Cosmic Microwave Background (CMB) radiation and the big bang itself.

Someone living on a world thirteen billion light-years away from us will have his or her own observable universe. By looking in one direction, he or she will see our own region of the universe in its earliest days. If that being looks the opposite way, he or she will see galaxies that are forever beyond our sight. Theoretically, these overlapping "observable universes" could go on forever, but can they?

The key to this mystery lies in Albert Einstein's famous General Theory of Relativity (*see box, page 32*). His theory shows that space and time can curve and warp in strange ways due to the presence of matter (and the gravity of this matter). The warping means that space can curve back on itself, so if you could keep going in a straight line, through several "observable universes," you would end up where you started.

According to this theory, if you could stand and gaze out on the horizon long enough, space would curve back around, allowing you to eventually see the back of your own head!

Most "supermassive" black holes are starved of new material to swallow. But when there is material within reach, the black hole can tear it to pieces and heat it up as it falls to its doom, spitting out jets of material from its poles.

EINSTEIN AND RELATIVITY

Albert Einstein (1879–1955) was considered a genius, and he rewrote many of the laws of physics at the beginning of the 1900s. His theories of relativity form the basis of all modern physics and cosmology.

Einstein confronted a major problem with traditional physics—the fact that light, and all other electromagnetic radiation, always travels at the same speed regardless of the direction in which its source moves. Based on this simple rule, Einstein investigated what happens to an object moving at close to the speed of light. He discovered that—as an object approaches the speed of light—time passes more slowly, the object becomes squashed along its direction of travel, and gains mass. This is called Einstein's 1905 Special Theory of Relativity. He followed it up in 1915 with the General Theory of Relativity, which explains the nature of space and time, and shows how large masses such as stars and planets distort the universe around them. Although they sometimes seem to contradict what our senses tell us in the everyday world, Einstein's theories have helped explain other theories in many different aspects of physics and astronomy.

Black holes and wormholes

Black holes are probably the most bizarre objects in astronomy. We believe they form when a giant star reaches the end of its life in a supernova explosion, and its core collapses into a super-dense stellar remnant. Normally, supernovae leave behind neutron stars (*see Chapter 2*), but if the star's core weighs more than about five Suns, its gravity will be so powerful that even the repulsive force between its neutrons will be unable to stop the core's collapse. Instead, the neutrons will be shredded into individual quarks, and the core will continue shrinking, with its gravity growing more powerful the smaller it gets. At a certain radius, the gravity on the star's surface will be so strong that nothing—not even light—can escape it. The core continues to shrink to an infinitely dense point in space and time called a singularity, and is forever sealed off from the rest of the universe by a barrier called the event horizon. No radiation can escape from the core into the rest of the universe, and any passing object that enters the event horizon will never return. The star's core has become a black hole in space and time.

Because they produce no light, black holes are hard to detect, but astronomers have found them through the effects these objects have on nearby stars. They have also found that huge "supermassive" black holes, with the mass of millions of Suns, lurk in the heart of many galaxies, including our own.

Black holes could offer a theoretical shortcut across space, allowing spaceships from an advanced civilization to jump from one part of the universe to another without having to actually travel faster than light. In 1985, U.S. cosmologist Kip Thorne (b. 1940) suggested this idea to his friend, U.S. planetary scientist Carl Sagan (1934–1996), to use in a science-fiction novel. According to Einstein's General Theory of Relativity, black holes are linked to other regions of space-time, but passing through the black hole is impossible because of the singularity at the center. Thorne suggested that, if an advanced

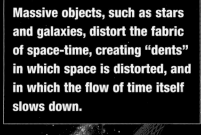

Massive objects, such as stars and galaxies, distort the fabric of space-time, creating "dents" in which space is distorted, and in which the flow of time itself slows down.

To understand how black holes and wormholes work, picture the universe as a flexible sheet, or— as in this case—a ball, curving back around on itself. Movement through normal space and time would involve moving on the surface of the ball.

A superdense black hole is like a funnel that drains energy and matter from the universe. In the singularity at its heart, normal space-time laws cease to apply. Singularities form theoretical "bridges" between different parts of the universe.

In a hypothetical wormhole, the throats of two black holes open so that a space traveler can pass through without being crushed in the singularity. The result is a near-instantaneous journey from one part of the universe to another.

alien race could build an antigravity device, they might be able to hold open the black hole's "throat." That would allow spaceships to fly around the singularity by creating a "wormhole" between two different parts of the universe. Thorne went on to explain how a wormhole could, in theory, be turned into a time machine without breaking the laws of physics.

Dark matter and the missing mass

One of the most important cosmological questions, "How much does the universe weigh?"

seems simple. The reason it is so important is that the amount of mass in the universe determines its gravity, which in turn could decide the ultimate fate of the universe. The reason it is such a difficult question to answer brings up another intriguing aspect of the universe: Most of the matter in the universe seems to be invisible.

Only the stars, some nebulae, and other hot objects give out visible light, so we might expect to find a lot of invisible material in the universe.

But today's telescopes can detect radio and infrared radiation from objects far too cool to shine visibly (dark clouds of gas and dust, faint dwarf stars, and others). Any material that cannot be detected by our instruments must actually be very strange—astronomers have given it the name "dark matter."

Dark matter makes its presence felt only by its gravity (*see box, page 35*), but this suggests that dark matter outweighs normal matter in the universe by nine to one. In other words, 90 percent of all the matter in the universe may be dark matter. For this reason, it is sometimes called the "missing mass." Astronomers think that dark matter is probably made up of two different types of material, which they have nicknamed MACHOs and WIMPs.

Astronomers usually gather information from distant objects by detecting radiation, normally in the form of visible light and infrared (heat) radiation. MACHOs (short for MAssive Compact Halo Objects) are large objects so dark or cold that even the most sensitive detectors cannot pick them up. They may lurk in the spherical and apparently empty "halos" around spiral galaxies. Possible MACHOs

Anyone journeying into a black hole would see their view of the universe become increasingly distorted. As they approached the singularity, space and time around them would become increasingly warped.

The curving of space-time around a black hole becomes increasingly steep closer to its center. At a certain radius, it becomes so steep that nothing, not even light, can escape. This is the event horizon—the visible surface of the black hole.

As you fell into a black hole, the difference in gravitational pull between your feet and head would stretch you out and eventually shred you into atoms—a process called "spaghettification."

According to Stephen Hawking, no information can escape from a black hole, but black holes can produce a form of radiation called Hawking Radiation. This allows black holes to lose energy and mass, until eventually, in the far future, they may "evaporate."

include stray planets, black dwarfs (white dwarf stellar remnants that have cooled until they no longer shine), and black holes. We know there are MACHOs in our own galaxy's halo (in the form of black holes). These have been detected by the way they distort the light of distant galaxies behind them. In general, this type of material probably makes up less than 20 percent of all the dark matter in the universe.

WIMPs (short for Weakly Interactive Massive Particles) are possible new types of particle that simply do not interact with normal matter, but yet have enough mass to account for most of the dark matter. This makes them extremely difficult to detect. One type of WIMP—the neutrino—has been found. A neutrino is a type of particle produced in huge numbers by the nuclear reactions inside stars. Neutrinos can pass through just about anything. Physicists observe neutrinos using massive tanks of chemicals surrounded by detectors and buried deep underground where other particles cannot penetrate. For a long time, neutrinos were thought to be completely massless. In 1998, U.S. and Japanese physicists proved that neutrinos have a tiny mass—and that there are so many neutrinos in the universe that they could account for a small fraction of the missing mass.

EVIDENCE FOR DARK MATTER

The evidence for the huge amounts of dark matter in the universe comes from the behavior of some of the objects we can see. Spiral galaxies, for example, rotate as the stars within them orbit the center of the galaxy. The mass of this type of galaxy is relatively spread out across its disk, so the overall rotation rate is not the same as it would be if all the mass were in the center. Astronomers measure the speed of rotation of different galaxies to calculate how the mass is spread out. They often find apparently huge amounts of invisible matter beyond the visible edge of the galaxies.

Similarly, astronomers can calculate the overall mass of galaxy clusters from the way the individual galaxies move. They often discover that the galaxies move as if there is a huge concentration of invisible mass at the center of the entire cluster.

This sequence of star images from the large Magellanic Cloud, a nearby small galaxy to our own Milky Way, is conclusive evidence for dark matter in an otherwise apparently empty "halo" region. In the center image below, "gravitational lensing" causes a sudden brightening of one star (arrow). As a dark, dense MACHO passes in front of that star, gravitational lensing briefly bends the light of the star toward Earth, magnifying and brightening the star's image from our viewpoint.

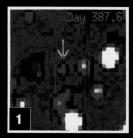
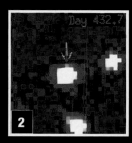
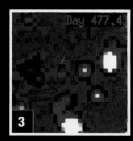

Dark energy and the fate of the universe

Cosmologists need to know the total mass of the universe in order to determine the effect of its gravity and its ultimate fate. Today, the universe is expanding rapidly. This is unlikely to change for trillions of years, but if gravity is strong enough, the expansion might eventually start to slow down. The universe might reach a balance where expansion slows but never quite stops. It could also be thrown into reverse—contracting and growing denser and hotter—before eventually ending in a "big crunch." Cosmologists refer to the alternative, in which the universe expands forever until the last stars burn out and even galaxies disintegrate, as the "big chill."

An artist's impression of the big crunch— one possible fate of the universe, in which the current expansion is reversed, and all the galaxies are pulled back together toward an eventual fiery end.

THE SUPERNOVA COSMOLOGY PROJECT

The Supernova Cosmology Project is a survey that uses a new method to measure the expansion of the universe. Using the *Hubble Space Telescope*, astronomers are looking for supernovae in the most distant galaxies. Different types of supernova trail off from their maximum brightness in different ways, so it's easy to tell Type II supernovae (massive exploding stars) from Type I (white dwarfs collapsing into neutron stars—*see page 17*). Because a Type I supernova always reaches the same peak in true brightness, its brightness from Earth can be used to determine its distance. When the project team compared their distances to faraway galaxies with those suggested by the galaxy redshifts, they found that the galaxies are always farther away than the redshifts suggested, meaning that the universe's expansion must be accelerating.

Astronomer Saul Perlmutter, one of the scientists who worked on the Supernova Cosmology Project. The project's intention was simply to double-check the Hubble Constant. Instead, its scientists discovered a new and mysterious force at work in the universe.

In addition to knowing the mass of the universe, cosmologists need to know the Hubble Constant—the current rate of expansion (*see page 23*). When they calculated their most accurate values for both of these figures, it appeared that the universe was very close to the threshold between big crunch and big chill.

Then, in the late 1990s, cosmologists using a new technique to double-check the value of the Hubble Constant made a shocking discovery. A previously unsuspected force appears to be speeding up the expansion of the universe. This force, called "dark energy," is as mysterious as its name suggests. Cosmologists disagree about what it is, where it comes from, and what effect it will have on the future of the universe.

The latest measurements show that dark energy has increased throughout the history of the universe. Up until about six billion years ago, the rate of cosmic expansion was gradually slowing down. Since then the rate has accelerated, indicating that dark energy has grown stronger than gravity—the most influential force in the universe. Unless dark energy decreases again, the universe seems certain to end in an everlasting "big chill"—but there's still another awesome possibility: If dark energy continues to increase, it might eventually overcome gravity at small scales, and perhaps overcome the forces between atoms as well. Then, dark energy would tear apart space-time in a catastrophic "big rip."

CHAPTER 5

IS ANYBODY OUT THERE?

There is one astronomical mystery that has a deep impact on our image of ourselves and our place in the universe. The human race has come a long way from its belief that Earth is the center of everything to an understanding of our true location orbiting an average star in the outskirts of one among countless galaxies. Does the existence of life and intelligence make Earth unique, or is the universe filled with countless alien civilizations, millions of years more advanced than our own?

Life in the universe

In just the last few years, speculation about alien life has gone from the stuff of science fiction to a real science, known as "astrobiology." There have been several reasons for this change, including a series of discoveries and realizations that made many scientists take alien life seriously for the first time.

For one thing, biologists have been surprised to discover life on our own planet existing and even thriving in situations they once thought were far too hostile. In 1977, oceanographers discovered colonies of animals living around extremely hot deep-sea volcanic vents in the middle of the Pacific ocean. The body chemistry of these animals is based on chemical waste from the superhot vents. The discovery shocked biologists into thinking that life on Earth might actually have begun around these vents and migrated toward the sunlight at

SETI (Search for Extra Terrestrial Intelligence) Institute directors Frank Drake and Jill Tarter, pioneers of the search for life elsewhere in the universe, stand beneath the Arecibo radio telescope in Puerto Rico.

The discovery of giant tube worms many miles deep in the ocean proves that life can survive in incredibly hostile conditions. These worms draw nourishment from the chemicals released by submarine volcanic vents.

a later stage. More recently, biologists discovered colonies of bacteria around scalding hot geysers and within hot rocks buried deep below the ground. If life can survive in these conditions on Earth, then why not on other planets?

Despite these discoveries, biologists still have a relatively narrow view of where life can develop. Most astrobiologists believe that life elsewhere in the universe will almost certainly develop from carbon-based "organic" chemicals because carbon has a unique ability to form large and complex molecules with other elements such as oxygen and hydrogen. Life—whatever form it takes—requires large molecules.

Life-forms also require a solvent—a stable liquid in which organic chemicals can dissolve and move around, contacting other molecules to form more complex structures. Water is the most likely solvent. It is plentiful in the universe, stays liquid over a wide range of temperatures, and does not destroy organic molecules through chemical reactions. We know from our own solar system, however, that liquid water is stable in just a few places, such as on the surface of Earth, and probably in the underground oceans on several of Jupiter's moons.

Although these conditions impose limits on where life can develop in the first place, living organisms are supremely adaptable and can survive in situations that are hostile to new life-forms. Some bacteria can survive high doses of radiation, temperatures well below freezing or far above boiling, and even prolonged periods in a vacuum. It's possible that simple organisms might be able to survive a journey through space, blasted off one planet among the rocks from a meteorite impact, only to fall on another planet at a later time. Some astronomers have suggested that primitive life could be carried around the galaxy deep-frozen inside comets. This idea, which suggests that life could be widespread in the universe and that life on Earth could have come from space, is called "Panspermia."

The Drake Equation

Although biologists can give us some ideas about where to look for life, it's still up to astronomers to find planets with suitable conditions. In 1961, Frank Drake, one of the pioneers of SETI (the Search for Extra-Terrestrial Intelligence program—see page 42) developed a simple

CARL SAGAN

U.S. astronomer Carl Sagan (1934-1996) was a planetary scientist and one of the first people to look seriously at the prospects for alien life in the universe (see also page 32). He worked with NASA on several space probes, including the Pioneer and Mariner missions, and came up with the idea of sending a message to the universe on board spacecraft that were leaving the solar system. This led to the engraved plaques mounted on

equation that allows us to estimate the likelihood that life—including the possibility of intelligent life—might exist in our galaxy. The Drake Equation appears below:

$$N = R \times f_p \times n_e \times f_i \times f_i \times f_c \times L$$

N is the number of civilizations in the galaxy today capable of communicating with others
R is the number of sunlike stars being born in our galaxy in a single year. (Sunlike stars are those able to shine steadily long enough to give rise to intelligent life on their planets.)
f_p is the fraction of those stars that develop a planetary system
n_e is the average number of habitable planets in each system
f_i is the fraction of those suitable planets on which life actually begins
f_i is the fraction of planets with life on which intelligence evolves
f_c is the proportion of planets on which intelligent life survives long enough to attempt communication with the rest of the galaxy
L is the average of lifetime of a "communicating civilization"

The Drake Equation clearly depends heavily on guesswork, and is more of a "thought experiment" than a mathematical tool. The main problem is that, so far, we have just one example on which to base all our thinking—our own planet. We can now make educated guesses at R and f_p, but the longer we contemplate the elements of the equation, the more questions that arise.

What exactly makes a planet suitable for life, for example? Some people argue that Earth's huge Moon helps protect life on Earth, and since our Moon appears to be a cosmic fluke, life-bearing planets should be similarly rare. Others think that the life around Earth's volcanic vents massively increases the possibilities that life could evolve on a number of planets and moons.

Perhaps the biggest mysteries, though, surround f_i and f_i. Even if the conditions for life are widespread in the universe, will life-forms automatically appear wherever conditions are right? Or is life as we know it exceedingly rare? A famous experiment conducted by scientists Stanley Miller (b. 1930) and Harold Urey (1893–1981) in 1953 suggests the opposite. They created a "model" of the early Earth in a

Pioneer 10 and *Pioneer 11,* and the gold disks carried by the Voyager space probes.

Sagan was among the first to suggest that Jupiter's moon Europa might have an ocean, and that Saturn's moon Titan could have lakes of methane. He studied the atmospheres of Venus and Mars, and drew parallels with Earth. He was also well-known to the public as host of the popular television series *Cosmos*, and as the author of many books on space and other scientific subjects.

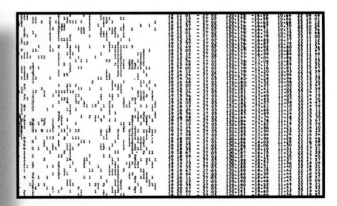

The computer printout of the so-called "Wow" signal—a distinct and apparently artificial signal detected in 1977 by the "Big Ear" radio telescope near Delaware, Ohio. Astronomer Jerry Ehman was so impressed by this signal that he wrote "Wow!" in the margin. Unfortunately, the signal never repeated itself, and has never been properly explained.

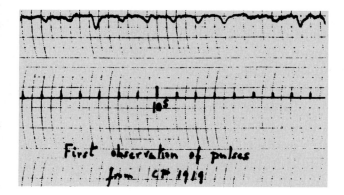

First observation of pulses from CP 1919

In 1967, astronomers detected this repeating signal from a region of the sky in the constellation Vulpecula. They seriously considered the idea that it might be an artificial signal, before realizing that they had actually discovered a rapidly spinning stellar remnant—the first pulsar.

laboratory flask. After just a few days, primitive organic chemicals began forming advanced amino acids—the building blocks of protein—vital for life.

And what about intelligence? Life-forms successfully existed for several billion years without highly evolved brains. Humans and our relatives have only appeared in the last few million years of Earth's 4.5-billion-year history.

From our own experience, the ability to possibly communicate with aliens comes at the same point in intellectual history that our species also has learned how to wipe itself out completely.

All of this means that the Drake Equation is open to almost any answer. Pessimists suggest that the value of R is 1—Earth is the only intelligent civilization in our galaxy. Optimists put the value much higher. In reality, the only way we will know for sure is if and when we find the signs of alien intelligence—and astronomers are already looking.

SIFTING THE DATA

Sorting through the huge amounts of radio "noise" that a radio telescope records as it scans the sky is a huge task. A complicated math technique called a "fast Fourier transform" can reveal hidden patterns in a record of radio noise, but the only way to do it quickly is with a computer. Yet even the most powerful single computer could take thousands of years to sift the noise from the entire sky for the faint signal from a distant world.

Fortunately, SETI researchers at the University of California at Berkeley came up with an ingenious solution to the problem of data overload, known as SETI@home. This is a small computer program that can be downloaded over the Internet. Once set up, it downloads "packets" of radio data sent out from a central computer. When a personal computer is unused for a short time, it processes the data, looking for anything that might be worth further investigation and displays its progress as a screensaver. When one data packet is finished, the program returns its results to the central SETI@home computer and downloads the next packet.

Thousands of people around the world have joined the project since it began, donating millions of hours of computing time. An alien signal remains elusive.

Searching for E.T.

How would an alien civilization make contact with us? The most obvious way would be by broadcasting a signal at radio wavelengths. Such a signal could be broadcast like a television signal so that anyone within range could pick it up. Or, they could beam it toward a specific location where they suspected listeners might be waiting. A targeted signal has one major advantage over a broadcast one—it requires much less power to travel much greater distances. The strength of a broadcast signal falls away rapidly as you get further from the transmitter, and every time you double your distance from it, it gets four times weaker.

Despite these problems, radio signals are such an obvious way of communicating that most of today's SETI research is focused on scanning the skies to look for patterns. Of course, in order to listen to a radio signal, you need to know its wavelength. Without that information, the search is even more like looking for a needle in a haystack. SETI researchers have decided to focus on a particular wavelength. They chose the 21-centimeter wavelength emitted by hydrogen, the simplest element. It can be produced by a relatively low-power transmitter, and is able to pass through dust clouds that would block signals in visible light. Because we do not know how the aliens' minds might work, the best we can hope for is that their civilization also realizes that they must send their signals on a fundamental wavelength. Researchers faced a similar problem of "thinking alien" when devising humanity's own first messages to the stars (*see page 45*).

Of course, radio signals are not the only way to detect an alien civilization. Very advanced aliens with the ability to manipulate stars might produce signals or other accidental signs of their presence

SETI@home allows amateur scientists worldwide to contribute to the search for extraterrestrial life. Participants run a screensaver computer program that analyzes SETI data collected by the "big science" radio telescopes, such as the VLA (Very Large Array) observatory near Socorro, New Mexico.

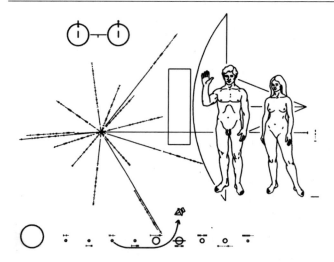

The plaques carried by the Pioneer space probes show male and female humans, a representation of the spacecraft, and a map of our solar system.

that we could detect with ordinary telescopes. Several types of exotic star have been suggested as the work of aliens when first discovered, but astronomers have found possible natural explanations for each. For example, the first pulsar, discovered in 1967 by its rapidly pulsing radio signal, was jokingly nicknamed "LGM-1" (short for Little Green Men). This discovery was

Physicist Freeman Dyson has suggested that an advanced civilization might "cage" their star in an object called a "Dyson sphere" in order to capture and use all of its energy. Dyson spheres would have a distinctive effect on a star's light and are one type of object that SETI astronomers are seeking.

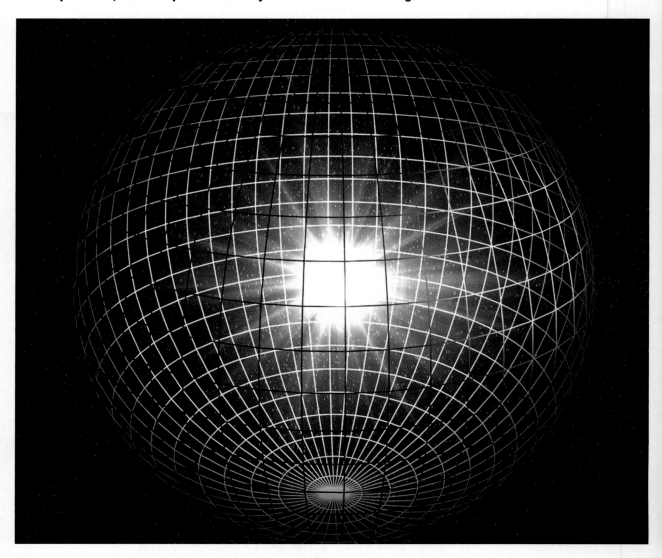

not publicly announced until the team had figured out that the pulsar had a natural origin.

Unless our current laws of physics are mistaken, or the aliens find a shortcut around them, it's very unlikely that we will ever meet them physically. The next best thing would be to find a piece of their technology, perhaps a robot probe similar to the ones we have already sent out of our solar system. The famous film *2001: A Space Odyssey* (1968) is based on the idea that aliens might send automatic "sentinels" to watch over promising planets and report back when life crosses a threshold of intelligence. A recent study showed that, because of the way that radio waves spread out and weaken as they get further from their source, a fleet of probes would actually require far less energy and effort than broadcasting a radio signal across a large region of space.

THE ARECIBO MESSAGE

In 1974, SETI astronomers transmitted humanity's first deliberate message into space from the giant Arecibo radio telescope in Puerto Rico. They devised an ingenious way of ensuring that the message could be decoded by any intelligent species that intercepts it. They sent the signal in binary code, a series of zeros and ones—the same language used by computers.

The three-minute message is still traveling at the speed of light toward a cluster of three hundred thousand stars that lies about twenty-five thousand light-years away from Earth.

Unfortunately, because of the natural rotation of our Milky Way galaxy, this target star cluster, known as the Great Cluster in Hercules, Messier 13, is also moving through the universe. So, by the time our radio message arrives at its target destination, Messier 13 will be long gone and in another part of the Milky Way.

Unless "someone else" happens to be in the area to receive our message, it will continue traveling for millions of years to the outer reaches of the universe. While radio signals leave Earth daily, we have not sent any other "formal" messages into outer space for more than thirty years.

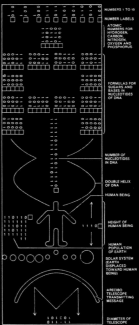

The binary message includes (top to bottom) information about the basic elements of life, the structure of DNA, a human silhouette, a diagram of our solar system, and an image of the Arecibo telescope.

GLOSSARY

amino acids: the building blocks of proteins that are vital to all living cells.

bacteria: tiny, single-celled organisms that can multiply quickly within another organism or substance, often to cause disease; many types of bacteria pose a threat to human health.

blueshift: a physical shifting of visible starlight toward the shorter, or "blue," end of wavelengths of the electromagnetic spectrum.

comet: a mass consisting of ice, rock, and dust that travels through space in a regular orbit. A comet passing the Sun usually develops a long "tail" of defrosted gases and particles.

conspiracy theory: a theory used to explain an event or certain set of circumstances caused by a secret plan by an unknown person or group with power.

Doppler effect: the noticeable change that occurs in the wavelength or frequency of light or sound, respectively, as it moves toward or away from a stationary observer.

electromagnetic radiation: any of the various wavelengths of mostly invisible rays emitted by stars.

fluke: a chance event.

infrared: an invisible form of long-wavelength radiation given off by hot objects; also called heat radiation.

ionize: to cause an object to take on a positive or negative charge; ionizing radiation can change organic matter and cause damage or even death.

magnetic pole: either of two small areas of concentrated magnetic force, one located in each polar area of an object's northern and southern hemispheres.

meteorite: a space object that enters and passes through Earth's atmosphere and strikes the ground.

optical illusion: an apparent image that does not convey a realistic representation of an object or scene.

primeval: of or relating to the earliest ages of human history; existing since the beginning of time.

pulsar: a rapidly rotating star that emits timed bursts of radiative energy as it spins.

quantum: extremely small units, or subdivisions, of energy.

redshift: a physical shifting of visible starlight toward the longer, or "red," end of wavelengths in the electromagnetic spectrum.

subatomic: relating to the inside of an atom, or to particles smaller than atoms.

terrestrial: belonging to the group of "rocky" planets that are similar to Earth in density and composition. In our solar system, Mercury, Venus, Earth, and Mars are known as the terrestrial planets.

ultraviolet: damaging (ionizing), invisible electromagnetic radiation with wavelengths shorter than visible light but longer than X-rays.

vacuum: an area completely empty of matter, including air; scientists can create a vacuum artificially by pumping all the air out of a sealed space. Outer space is considered a vacuum.

FURTHER INFORMATION

BOOKS

Bredeson, Carmen. *NASA Planetary Spacecraft: Galileo, Magellan, Pathfinder, and Voyager.*
    Countdown to Space (series). Enslow (2000).
Chrismer, Melanie. *Highlights from the Hubble Telescope: Postcards from Space.*
    Countdown to Space (series). Enslow (2003).
Dinwiddie, Robert, et. al. *Universe: The Definitive Visual Guide.* DK (2005).
Gribbin, John. *Time & Space.* Eyewitness Books. DK Children (2000).
Hantula, Richard. *Exploring Outer Space.* Isaac Asimov's 21st Century Library of the Universe (series).
    Gareth Stevens (2005).
Kerrod, Robin. *Space Probes.* The History of Space Exploration (series). World Almanac® Library (2004).
Rau, Dana Meachen. *Black Holes.* Our Solar System (series). Compass Point Books (2005).

WEB SITES

www.nasa.gov
Visit NASA's homepage and access information about the latest missions and activities.

www.space.com
Surf a great Web site for daily space news.

http://hubblesite.org/
Tour the universe with a little help from the *Hubble Space Telescope*.

http://curious.astro.cornell.edu/index.php
Submit space-related questions to and read answers from Cornell University's astronomy department.

http://setiathome.berkeley.edu
Learn more about the search for extraterrestrial intelligence.

Publisher's note to educators and parents: Our editors have carefully reviewed these Web sites to ensure that they are suitable for children. Many Web sites change frequently, however, and we cannot guarantee that a site's future contents will continue to meet our high standards of quality and educational value. Be advised that children should be closely supervised whenever they access the Internet.

INDEX